TELL ME ABOUT
MEASURES

TELL ME ABOUT
MEASURES

By ALAIN GRÉE
Pictures by GÉRARD GRÉE

Translated from the French by ALEXANDRA CHAPMAN

Library of Congress Catalog Card Number: 75-179405
ISBN: 0-448-02936-7 (Trade Edition)
ISBN: 0-448-04469-2 (Library Edition)

Translation copyright © 1972, by CASTERMAN, Paris.   Originally published in
French under the title *Petit Tom Veut Tout Mesurer,* © 1969, CASTERMAN, Paris.
Published pursuant to agreement with CASTERMAN, Paris.
Not for sale in the British Commonwealth, except Canada.

GROSSET & DUNLAP • Publishers • NEW YORK
A NATIONAL GENERAL COMPANY

Tommy likes to find out how tall his friends are and how much they weigh.
"Johnny has grown," says Tommy.
"He's as tall as you," adds Susan.

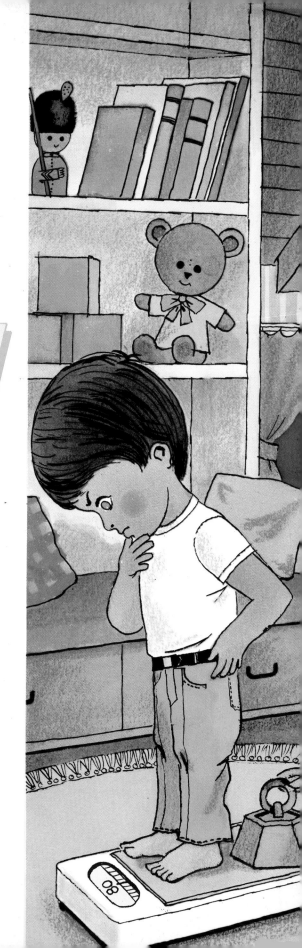

Tommy

JAN. 1: 3 ft. 8 in.
JUNE 15: 3 ft. 10 in.

Susan

JAN. 1: 3 ft. 5 in.
JUNE 15: 3 ft. 7 in.

Johnny

JAN. 1: 3 ft. 7 in.
JUNE 15: 3 ft. 10 in.

Who was the tallest on January 1?
Who was the tallest on June 15?

7 o'clock: I brush my teeth.

Noon: I have lunch at home.

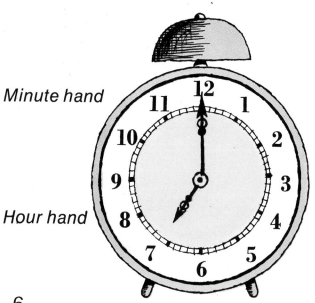

Minute hand

Hour hand

The big hand of the clock moves and shows the minutes. It goes around the clock in one hour, or 60 minutes.

The little hand shows the hours. The hours have these numbers:

1 2 3 4 5 6 7 8 9 10 11 12

During the day the hands go all around the clock. At night, too. Twelve (12) hours during the day, and twelve (12) hours during the night.

6

5 o'clock: I go for a ride.

9 o'clock: I am asleep.

Tommy can tell time.
His days are filled with things to do.
At seven o'clock, he gets up.
At eight o'clock, he eats breakfast.
At eight-thirty — half-past eight — he walks to school.
At noon, he eats lunch.
At four-thirty — half-past four — he has cookies and milk.
At five o'clock, he rides his bicycle.

At six o'clock, he eats his evening meal.
At seven-thirty — half-past seven — he looks through his picture book.
By nine o'clock, he is fast asleep.

The days of the week:

Sunday	Thursday
Monday	Friday
Tuesday	Saturday
Wednesday	

The months of the year:

January	April	July	October
February	May	August	November
March	June	September	December

It's vacation time! No one has thought of anything else for a week. There will be new things to see, and time for games, and fun, and good things to eat.

The family is almost ready to start on the trip. Some of the suitcases have been packed for days. But Tommy always finds something more he would like to take along.

The family will be away for a month. A month is thirty days. It is also four weeks.

Father is worried. The car may not hold everything!

1 gallon
(4 quarts)

1 quart
(2 pints)

1 pint
(2 cups)

1 cup

Today Mother is going to make pancakes for breakfast. Tommy prepares the batter. Eggs and flour are mixed together. But how will Tommy measure two cups of milk? Tommy uses a measuring cup.

There! Now the pancakes are cooking — a sugared one for Susan, a thin one for the cat, and a small one for Mother.

Tommy thinks it's possible to catch pancakes in the air with a butterfly net!

Brrr! It's cold! But Tommy's friends are out in the snow, gathering large chunks of it to build a snowman. The snowman gets a hat, a mustache, and a pipe. He looks across the white fields with his black coal eyes.

"Watch out! Tommy's coming down the hill on his sled!"

Yes, Tommy was surprised to see the snowman. It was right in his path as he came down the hill.

SUMMER

The sky is blue.
There are no clouds.
The sun shines and
it is very warm.

AUTUMN

Clouds hide the sun.
It is cooler. The
thermometer reads 50°F
Put on a sweater!

WINTER

Brrr! The sky is gray.
The thermometer has
dropped to below
freezing. It will snow.

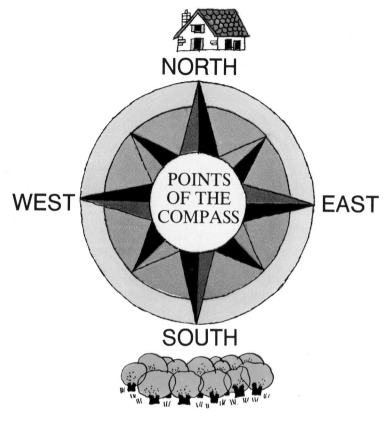

NORTH

WEST

POINTS
OF THE
COMPASS

EAST

SOUTH

The compass Tommy holds in his hand shows four main points: north, south, east and west. The needle of the compass always points to the northern part of the earth.

Tommy's home is north of the forest. The forest is south of his home. In what direction must Tommy and Susan walk to get back home?

Susan thinks they must go toward the south.

Tommy looks at his compass.

"No," he tells his sister. "We must walk in that direction — toward the north."

Tommy likes to travel. He often day-dreams about the places he will visit when he is big. A touch of the starter, and—wonder of wonders!—he's off at the wheel of his make-believe car. Only trains and airplanes can go faster.

But be careful, Tommy. The best driver is not the fastest one, but the one who never has an accident.

The walking boy can travel 3 miles in one hour. He walks 3 miles an hour. The car can travel 60 miles in one hour. It moves 60 miles an hour. The train can travel 100 miles in one hour. It moves 100 miles an hour. The airplane can travel 600 miles in one hour. How fast does it fly?

Tommy does errands for his mother. He likes to go shopping. Today his mother needs two pineapples, some tomatoes, and three pounds of apples.

The grocer's wife puts some weights on one side of a scale. The weights on

1 pound = 16 ounces

16 ounces = 1 pound

the scale will be the same as three pounds. The scales will balance when three pounds of apples are put on the other side of the scale.

Father has just built a doghouse for Lucky. It seems to be a fine doghouse, but . . .

The doghouse is too small.

Lucky is too big.

Lucky can't fit in the doghouse.

Tommy takes a tape measure an stretches it out.

"From back to front, the doghous measures exactly 36 inches," say Tommy.

"Yes—and Lucky measures 46 inches

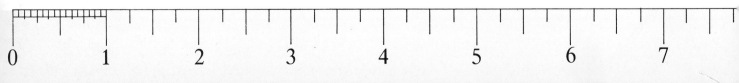

from head to tail," adds Susan.

There's no doubt about it—Lucky must have a larger doghouse.

Lucky doesn't mind. Tonight he'll sleep at the foot of Tommy's bed.

3 feet=1 yard

12 inches=1 foot

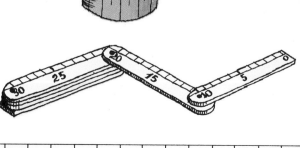